Where Egos Dare

Where Egos Dare

How a House Church Brought Me Back to Christ

GLENN H. GOREE

Foreword by Norman Goodyear
Foreword by Owen R. Keiser

RESOURCE *Publications* · Eugene, Oregon

WHERE EGOS DARE
How a House Church Brought Me Back to Christ

Resource Publications
An Imprint of Wipf and Stock Publishers
199 W. 8th Ave., Suite 3
Eugene, OR 97401

www.wipfandstock.com

PAPERBACK ISBN: 978-1-5326-1581-8
HARDCOVER ISBN: 978-1-5326-1583-2
EBOOK ISBN: 978-1-5326-1582-5

Manufactured in the U.S.A.   JANUARY 20, 2017

Synonyms for dedication are devotion, commitment, enthusiasm, keenness, perseverance, allegiance, loyalty, and staunchness. I can think of no better words of love to describe my Ecclesia, my Life Group. These variant shades of meaning unite to define the love I feel for my house church. And it is with the same love they bestow on me each week that I devote this publication to them.

Contents

CONTENTS

Foreword
by Norman Goodyear

MY FIRST ORGANIZED SMALL-GROUP experience was in 1992 at the home of Glenn and Valerie Goree. We met for a time, but, like most things in this fallen world, it slowly ended. There were new jobs, military reassignments, aging parents, a death, and Glenn—who you'll soon discover in the pages that follow—went 'missing in action.' The group dissolved. Even so, I still fondly remember the relationships cultivated then, that still continue to this day.

My wife and I began attending another small group in 1998 when we moved to a new area of town. A few years later, we invited Glenn to visit our new group, knowing little of his intervening journey. In this group we had found a refuge, a family, a home. So did Glenn.

I can only echo Glenn's perspective on our intimate attachment to this life group. It is our family. It is our Ecclesia. And although we attend a 'brick and mortar' building on Sunday morning, this group is our church.

In this book Glenn calls us to Ecclesia. Intimate fellowship. Devotion to prayer. Courage to act. My prayer is that the reader may find an Ecclesia of fellowship that is devoted to the Lord Jesus Christ and to prayer. There you will find the Spirit of power and love and self-control.

> "God gave us a spirit not of fear but of power and love and self-control."
> II Timothy 1:7

San Antonio, Texas
November 2016

Foreword

by Owen R. Keiser

IN GLENN'S LATEST BOOK, *Where Egos Dare,* he describes the intimacy and honesty of his Christian Life Group. Through a series of poems, he plumbs the depths of the original church, and compares that to the Life Group which is composed of members that are diverse in background but united in striving to learn more of God, to become more Christ-like in their daily walk, and to support one another. While a brick and mortar church has an important place as a source of corporate worship and instruction, it is in the small group setting where Scripture can be intimately discussed, studied, understood, and applied.

While each small group is unique, Glenn describes how his experience can be used for others attempting to replicate the essence of the early church. Glenn's insight will be useful to groups, both old and new, attempting to minister to their members with love and understanding.

November 2016
San Antonio, TX

Acknowledgments

VALERIE GOREE, MY WIFE, deserves special recognition for polishing the thoughts expressed in this brief volume. If it were not for her keen eye for detail, and for sharpening my ideas, none of my works would be considered, much less published. "As iron sharpens iron, so one man sharpens another." (Proverbs 27:17) Valerie sharpens my writing, my life, and my soul. No man has been blessed with a better wife, friend, and companion.

PART I

Introduction

CHURCH—THE BUILDING OR THE worshipers?

Ecclesia? Doesn't it mean the same as *church*?

The words are synonymous now, but that's not the original meaning of the English word *Ecclesia*.

We derive our word from the Greek *ekklesia*, a *called out* group, which means assembly, congregation, council, or convocation, a large formal assembly of people. Originally, the Greeks used the word to describe a meeting of citizens, especially the public assemblies of ancient Athens. The word was also used to describe an unruly gathering of men.

The early church used Ecclesia to refer to their gatherings of Christians. However, over time, English versions of the Bible have translated the word as *church*. It is interesting to note that the word for *church* was not used in the original texts of the New Testament.

As the numbers of Christians grew during the first century, they met in homes, graveyards, catacombs, fields, or on hillsides—any place where they felt safe from being arrested by the Romans.

At first, the construction of a church was nothing more than knocking out a wall in a house so that a congregation of fifteen or more could easily assemble. We can only imagine, that as time passed, the idea of constructing a dedicated building for worship developed because the numbers of Christians increased. Hence, a central place for them to organize, gather, and administer was necessary.

In an article written by Everett Ferguson titled "Why and When did Christians Start Constructing Special Buildings for Worship?" featured in the magazine, *Christian History*, 2008, he states: "Unless claims for recent discoveries of early Christian meeting places are confirmed, the earliest building certainly devoted to Christian use is at Dura Europos on the Euphrates River in eastern Roman Syria. It was a house that came into Christian possession and was remodeled in the 240s. Two rooms were combined to form the assembly room, and another room became a baptistry—the only room decorated with pictures. Dura was destroyed by the Sassanian Persians in 256, so the house's use as a church was short-lived."

Early in the fourth century, Constantine declared the Christian faith the official state religion. It was from that point on that the number of believers multiplied, and the construction of church buildings increased in proportion to financial resources. The growth has continued for the last two thousand years, and has contributed to Christians' understanding of the word *church*—the building in which people worship, and the universal group of believers, regardless of denomination.

In the following chapters and poems, I use the word *Ecclesia* with its original meaning in mind.

1

I Once was Lost, but Now I'm Found

AFTER MANY YEARS OF faithful church attendance, and serving as a missionary and a minister, I lost my way and turned my back on organized religion. However, there was an ache in my soul, and eventually I began searching for a spiritual home. I returned to the congregation I'd left, but still felt a void in my spirit. And then, one day in 2004, an elder asked if I'd consider attending his Life Group. I agreed, half-heartedly, with no idea how this decision would change my life.

My Life Group, as I call it now, consists of eight to ten core couples. Over the years, individuals and couples have come and gone. We meet Sunday evenings at five o'clock. Different couples host the meetings, usually for a month at a time, September through May. We take a few weeks off for Christmas and New Year, and break for the summer months. There are two elders from traditional brick-and-mortar churches who serve as our elected leaders, one is the primary teacher who leads our Bible lessons.

The gathering is aptly named because it is our *Group* that gives us *Life.* Most of us are members of different congregations, but to me, my Life Group is my *Ecclesia.* Our simple gathering each week is taken straight out of the New Testament. Consider the following scriptures.

"They devoted themselves to the apostles' teaching and to the fellowship, to the breaking of bread and to prayer. Everyone was filled with awe, and many wonders and miraculous signs were done by the apostles. All the believers were together and had everything in common. Selling their possessions and goods, they gave to anyone as he had need. Every day they continued to meet together in the temple courts. They broke bread in their homes and ate together with glad and sincere hearts, praising God and enjoying the favor of all the people. And the Lord added to their number daily those who were being saved." (Acts 2:42–47)

Similar to the early church, we gather for a meal, usually potluck style. None of us leaves our Sunday evening gatherings hungry, either spiritually or physically. Like babies, we are filled with nourishing food, but also with the mother's milk of God's word, providing a balanced diet of the pure, rich nutrients and minerals of Biblical truth.

"How can a young man keep his way pure? By living according to your word. I seek you with all my heart; do not let me stray from your commands. I have hidden your word in my heart that I might not sin against you." (Psalm 119:9–10)

"Open my eyes that I may see wonderful things in your law. I am a stranger on earth; do not hide your commands from me. My soul is consumed with longing for your laws at all times." (Psalm 119:18–20)

"Teach me, O Lord, to follow your decrees; then I will keep them to the end." (Psalm 119:33)

"I have considered my ways and have turned my steps to your statutes. I will hasten and not delay to obey your commands. At midnight I rise to give you thanks for your righteous laws." (Psalm 119:59–60, 62)

We may read and study books written by Christian authors, but these are only manmade formulas. And just as there are many manmade baby formulas advertising they are better for infants, many physicians believe nothing can substitute the purity of a mother's milk. Similarly, there is no substitute for the pure milk found only in God's word.

But our weekly feeding is only a small part of what we share in Ecclesia fellowship. For you see we have been cradled in God's love by the Ecclesia of our close family of brethren. Sometimes I giggle as I drive home on Sunday nights. Why, you may ask? Just like a baby coos and giggles when he feels safe, secure, warm, protected, and accepted, that's how I've felt ever since I began my association with my Ecclesia in 2004.

Another comparison reminds me of the baby who senses that no matter what pain he may encounter, he can find solace in the embracing arms of his family. Like the buffalo used to form a circle around their young to protect them against wolf packs, so too does our Life Group encircle each member needing special, spiritual protection. When we pray, we are spiritual warriors who put the fear of God into Satan and his condemned followers. My Life Group has taught me over the years that prayer is the most powerful weapon we Christians have and that we don't utilize this tool enough.

The group has embraced another spiritual virtue to the max. No matter what the disobedience, not one soul in our family will judge or condemn, but instead accept and restore. Many times I heard, "I have struggled with that sin also."

Although we gather in one room for Bible study, prayer, and singing, there's an interesting custom we follow for our evening meal, a tradition dating back to early tribal man. The men and women sit in separate rooms while eating. As you well know this allows each group to talk about the other in safety and security, something husbands and wives need from time to time.

In the last few years we have started taking the Lord's Supper. Several years ago, some members of the group participated in a tour of the Holy Land. One of the sites we visited was the Garden Tomb in Jerusalem, a possible site for the Lord's crucifixion. While there, we were served the Lord's Supper, the wine in little cups carved from olive wood. One of the group purchased enough cups for us to use in our Life Group meetings. Now these little cups serve as a poignant reminder of Jesus' sacrifice every time we partake of the Lord's Supper which has become an integral part of our gathering.

The following chapters will explain why my Life Group has become my Ecclesia.

2

Intimacy

INTIMACY IS PERHAPS THE most fulfilling gift this group gives me. We have become so intimate that some visiting couples and individuals decided not to return. When we asked why, they explained they thought we were too personal. We revealed too many sins in our lives that they felt should not be discussed openly. They were embarrassed because of the depth of our intimacy. It was too much for them to handle.

But, as far as I'm concerned, intimacy is at the heart of our Christian faith. Consider the following Scripture.

"Brothers, if someone is caught in a sin, you who are spiritual should restore him gently. But watch yourself, or you also may be tempted. Carry each other's burdens, and in this way you will fulfill the law of Christ." (Galatians 6:1–2)

Over the past twelve years, we have developed a level of trust which allows us to share every detail, to withhold no issue from the group. We reveal the struggles we are having within our marriages, discuss our children, and, since most of us are over sixty, our grandchildren too. We share deep, personal struggles, finances, jobs, vacations, new ventures, and any other topic, positive or negative.

Our focus is not only inward, but we also share concerns about people in our lives such as friends outside our group, or neighbors who are sick, going through divorce, searching for jobs, or other immediate, critical needs.

Unlike many family units, we discuss our love for each other, embracing with a spiritual connection.

"Greet one another with a holy kiss. All the churches of Christ send greetings." (Romans 16:16)

"Greet one another with a holy kiss." (II Corinthians 13:12)

"Greet all the brothers with a holy kiss." (I Thessalonians 5:26)

All of the men in my Life Group mean more to me than my biological brother, and their wives are like the sisters I never had growing up as a child. I know that if I need any one of them, he or she would be at our home in a matter of minutes.

For example, many of the members attended our daughter's wedding. Several years before this beautiful event, a terrible tragedy befell our child. During a freak accident, she broke her leg. After nine surgeries over a two-year period, suffering through osteomyelitis—infection of the bone—she came close to losing her leg. The wife of one of our elders has a special gift of teaching, visiting, and encouraging. I will never forget the day she visited our daughter in the hospital after one of her surgeries. In Jesus' name, this holy woman got down on her knees next to our daughter's bed and prayed. At the end of her sacred prayer, she predicted our daughter would one day be married. And she prophesied she would dance at our daughter's wedding.

Three years later, she did just that.

Here is another example of our brotherly love. After participating in the group for eighteen months, I finally worked up the courage to tell them I was being treated for Hepatitis C, and had fallen away from the church for a number of years. I had realized God was using my illness to humble me, and thanked the group for how they had lifted my spirit.

You know what they did? They sat me in a chair and gathered around me in a circle of faith while each person placed a hand on my head or shoulders. Then they took turns praying over me and for me. I think I saw the gates of heaven open that night. I was given a glimpse of heaven that I will never forget. The experience allowed me to breathe its air, and feel the warmth of the Son on my face. For more than a decade I have been intoxicated by my Life Group's wine of pure love and devotion.

3

Prayer

PRAYER IS THE LIFEBLOOD of our Ecclesia. I never knew the true meaning nor the power of prayer until I began attending my Life Group. We pray for everything and anything, any time. In fact, I think some visitors have been repulsed by our excessive praying. At first, I felt the group's penchant for praying frequently and for every little thing was over the top. But let me show you what Paul wrote.

"Be joyful in hope, patient in affliction, faithful in prayer." (Romans 12:12)

"Do not be anxious about anything, but in everything, by prayer and petition, with thanksgiving, present your requests to God. And the peace of God, which transcends all understanding, will guard your hearts and your minds in Christ Jesus." (Philippians 4:6–7)

"Devote yourselves to prayer, being watchful and thankful. And prayer for us, too, that God may open a door for our message, so that we may proclaim the mystery of Christ, for which I am in chains. Pray that I may proclaim it clearly, as I should." (Colossians 4:2–4)

Before we partake in our meal, we gather in a large circle, hold hands, and pray. At the end of the evening, we repeat the process, but this time, one of the elders compiles a list of prayer requests. Then, as we pray, everyone is given the opportunity to speak whatever is on his or her heart.

Our prayer list is also e-mailed to the group within the next few days. So yep, you guessed it, we can include these requests in our prayers during the week.

Let me tell you what else has happened to me personally. My prayer life has increased exponentially. My wife and I pray together more than we used to, and I frequently pray at the places where I work as a contract counselor. I pray while I travel to and from the three offices I use, thanking God for green traffic lights, convenient parking places, and ask his forgiveness when I'm impatient with fellow motorists. I also have found over the years I have become a prayer opportunist.

What is a prayer opportunist? It's a person who looks for every opportunity to pray throughout the day, by himself, or with others. You might think I'm a little crazy, or a fanatic. That's okay, because before my participation in my Ecclesia, that was exactly what I thought of others who prayed at every opportunity.

4

Courage

COURAGE IS A VIRTUE I lacked before I became part of my Ecclesia. I was weak in my faith, and, to be truthful, embarrassed by spontaneously sharing my faith. However, after being part of my Ecclesia, I gained the courage to begin a practice that has lasted for ten years. As an onsite EAP counselor for a large financial organization, I see hundreds of employees. I started placing my Bible out on my desk each day. I never have to say anything about my faith. Employees who visit my office often ask if I will pray with them or read the Scriptures. Many have said that they were fearful of coming to a therapist's office, but were reassured when they walked in and saw a Bible on my desk and were immediately relieved and felt comfortable.

Just having my Bible visible has allowed me to pray and talk about Christ with thousands of people over the years I have been with this company. Most of the time, I see employees only once and then refer them out into our citywide network of contracted counselors. But these employees have had the Word of God dry the tears from their eyes, heal aching hearts, sooth bruised souls, and comfort battered spirits.

There is one final truth about my Bible on my desk that I had not anticipated. It has served not so much to tell others about Christ as it has served to remind me of who I am—a Christian, a follower of Christ.

5

Simplicity

SIMPLICITY IS PERHAPS THE most beautiful dynamic of our Life Group. Let me give you some examples. Over the years we have become involved in several missionary or humanitarian efforts. Sometimes a member will bring a worthy cause to our attention, or a representative from an organization will join us for a meal, and describe his or her work, local or far-a-field. Since we are just a group of like-minded Christians, there's no committee we have to convince, or formal process we have to follow. If we decide to act upon a proposal presented to us, then we do. If, on the other hand, some folks in our group don't want to participate, then there's no pressure to comply. No one gets angry or tries to persuade. Usually our decision is by vote, or individual choice, or a combination of both. Here again, we are following examples provided by the early church.

"Now about the collection for God's people: Do what I told the Galatian churches to do. On the first day of every week, each one of you should set aside a sum of money in keeping with his income, saving it up, so that when I come no collections will have to be made."
(I Corinthians 16:1–2)

There is also simplicity in our fellowship. Since we are a small group, there are no corporate levels of management deciding with whom we can interact, or which groups or individuals we can support. If someone within or outside of our Ecclesia needs help, then the need is brought to our collective attention, and we each do what we are financially able. We have no budget except what each person has in his or her heart and pocket. We have no motivation except how we can serve Christ. And finally, we have no goals except those placed in our hearts by our Lord and Savior.

Therefore, if you ask me why God prefers small groups, I think it's because their intimacy, prayer, courage, and simplicity are spiritual powder kegs. The first century church grew because the Holy Spirit was in charge, and it moved men's and women's hearts to act in the name of Jesus. They served without first checking with a pastor, or the head of a department, or the corporate church structure to see if they should. The first century church was powerful in the face of persecution because it was grass-roots strong. It grew because individuals and small groups acted spontaneously as they saw a need arise.

"What good is it, my brothers, if a man claims to have faith but has no deeds? Can such faith save him? Suppose a brother or sister is without clothes and daily food. If one of you says to him, 'Go, I wish you well; keep warm and well fed,' but does nothing about his physical needs, what good is it? In the same way, faith by itself, if it is not accompanied by action, is dead." (James 2:14–17)

My final thought is there's nothing inherently wrong with brick and mortar facilities. However, what is inherent in their nature is to become self-serving. By their design and corporate structure, they lend themselves to become the end and not a means to an end. Staff becomes more involved in *running* a church instead of *being* an Ecclesia.

Jesus said in Matthew 18:20 that when two or more are gathered together in his name he would be in their midst. The problem with human nature is that when these same two individuals come together to form a brick and mortar edifice, one or the other will have an innate need to be in charge. Could this same human imperfection be found in small, home churches? Of course. Both a small Ecclesia and a brick and mortar production are comprised of people who, by nature, are flawed. In my situation, I've been blessed to be part of an Ecclesia that is as close to heaven as mortals can be on this side of eternity. Through their example, I have a good idea of what heaven will be like, and they inspire me to live as close to Christ as I can.

PART II

Poems

BRICK AND MORTAR, OR ECCLESIA?

To whom or what do I call my soul's own?
'Tis not an imperfect mortal reached by telephone wire or vocal tone.

To whom or what do I pledge my eternal liege?
'Tis the one who scaled death's wall in resurrection's siege.

With whom or what will I one day gloriously ascend?
'Tis he whose right arm is strong and never bends.

Why, then, do we place our hope in brick and mortar,
In which successive generations venerate their charter?

What is it about stone and cement
That tends to overshadow one so perfect and heaven sent?

I think it's due to human nature's inherent need,
That seeks to be part of a family with an earthly parent seed.

Oh, Ecclesia, I hear your divine, perfect call
To be set apart and different from this earth's mortal chattel stall.

Keep my eyes focused on Golgotha's cruel but necessary cross,
That I may not be beguiled by brick and mortar's pride and loss.

∼

"When they came to the place called The Skull, there they cruci-
fied him, along with the criminal—one on his right, the other on
his left. Jesus said, 'Father, forgive them, for they do not know what
they are doing.' And they divided up his clothes by casting lots."

(Luke 23:33–34)

AROUND THE FAMILY TABLE

The men sat in one room, and the women in another,
Knowing that their bond in Jesus made them His sister and brother.

Then they gathered in a living room and circled in a group,
Ten to fifteen souls dreary from another week struggling in life's soup.

They sang, and prayed, then they studied God's word,
Knowing their Savior received in worship what He sweetly heard.

Smallness, closeness, intimacy, and love,
All found in weekly fellowship with a renewed focus on God above.

I think there's wisdom in what the early church practiced,
It wasn't by accident, but design that persecution made it difficult to access.

I wonder if the modern church of today
Wouldn't be better off in this ancient way.

Perhaps in small groups we'd find what we're missing,
That is a small family in whom we find love with hugs and kissing.

❧

"Every day they continued to meet together in the temple courts.
They broke bread in their homes and ate together with glad and
sincere hearts, praising God and enjoying the favor of all the
people."
(Acts 2:46–47)

JESUS'S BLOOD MAKES US STRONG

Who's in charge, it may be asked?
Who's been assigned what needs to be tasked?
In whose earthly light will our souls be basked?

Will it be him or her, and will we in our group concur,
And how will we make this decision from hearts astir?

Since there're only a few in this tiny house group,
Why not pray about it so God is kept in the loop?
Otherwise by Satan we may be duped.

Until such time we are direction given,
Let us all point our prayers and thoughts to the Divine One in heaven.

For it matters not whom we choose here below,
Because Jesus is our Savior in whom resides an eternal glow,
And I'm sure He will speak to our hearts about the decision He'll bestow.

Let us then worship each week in prayer and song,
That we together glorify Him whose blood made us strong.

∼

"Since we have now been justified by his blood, how much more
shall we be saved from God's wrath through him! For if, when we
were God's enemies, we were reconciled to him through the death
of his Son, how much more, having been reconciled, she we be
saved through his life!"
(Romans 5:9–10)

"In him we have redemption through his blood, the forgiveness of
sins, in accordance with the riches of God's grace that he lavished
on us with all wisdom and understanding."
(Ephesians 1:7–8)

WHERE EGOS DARE

Be no longer confused, my earth-bound feet,
But hasten your stride to crimson truth where earth and heaven meet.

Glory not in the temporal flags and banners circling the skies where egos dare,
Celebrating human edifices built in Jesus's name, because their designers care.

"See what we've done in the name of Christ our Lord and Savior,"
They say, patting backs. For this rich moment's grand opening they savor.

I pray, permit me this opportunity to perhaps query a little skeptical,
Are these monuments of costly stone for Jesus, or to make you feel special?

Have you examined your motives behind this architectural song?
Are its notes true to the Gospel's tune? Where do their lyrics belong?

Have you considered the tithe-equity in coin and treasure,
And thought how it could have fed empty stomachs to Satan's displeasure?

Again, I beg your pardon and forgiveness please,
But I think the prototype of the early church should bring us to our knees,

For it models not of marbled domes, air-cooled rooms with colorful fabric,
But of small assemblages in humble homes, freely offered, a choice sometimes tragic.

The wisdom of house churches is in front of every Christian's nose.
Read about the Tower of Babble and see where it goes,

Because it was built to the glory of man and not his maker,
As the motive for construction was hidden by pride's dark nature.

So what earthbound monument does God desire?
A broken heart and contrite spirit that to God self-effacingly aspire.

For in these stones are found eternal temples, majestic and indestructible,
And not in brick and mortar whose earthbound life is easily predictable.

~

"They said to each other, 'Come, let's make bricks and bake them thoroughly.' They used brick instead of stone, and tar instead of mortar. Then they said, 'Come, let us build ourselves a city, with a tower that reaches to the heavens, so that we may make a name for ourselves and not be scattered over the face of the whole earth.'"
(Genesis 11:3–4)

"When pride comes, then comes disgrace, but with humility comes wisdom."
(Proverbs 11:2)

"Pride goes before destruction, a haughty spirit before a fall."
(Proverbs 16:18)

"'But the tax collector stood at a distance. He would not even look up to heaven, but beat his breast and said, 'God, have mercy on me, a sinner.' 'I tell you that this man, rather than the other, went home justified before God. For everyone who exalts himself will be humbled, and he who humbles himself will be exalted."
(Luke 18:13–14)

"Do nothing out of selfish ambition or vain conceit, but in humility consider others better than yourselves."
(Philippians 2:3)

INTIMACY UNMATCHED

There's an appetite outside of what the body craves,
It's more essential than what food, shelter, and clothing staves,
Yes, it even inherently directs much of how mortals behave.

God shaped sinew and bone with a necessity,
That gives humans either obscure emptiness or spiritual ecstasy.

Intimacy is unequaled in all souls' desires,
To connect and touch with another flesh is what individuals aspire.

And yet there's a passion in the earthbound spirit,
That is deeper than having another finite being close and near it.

The utmost joining of husband and wife,
Pales, compared to this yearning, that seeks more than this short life.

An awareness of holy dimensions, other
Than four or five score that we live with our brother.

Yearning for a connection with the Holy Spirit eternal,
As it cries out pleading how to achieve this in the external.

The cross is the answer for all those who believe,
For it gives mankind what he can't achieve.

And God gave us the Ecclesia to fulfill this need
That the early church in their small groups did succeed.

Family soon takes on a unique and special meaning,
As with one another, both needs are filled in holy gleaning.

≈

"'I am the vine; you are the branches. If a man remains in me and I in him, he will bear much fruit; apart from me you can do nothing. If anyone does not remain in me, he is like a branch that is thrown away and withers; such branches are picked up, thrown into the fire and burned. If you remain in me and my words remain in you, ask whatever you wish, and it will be given you.'"

(John 15:5–7)

"'My prayer is not for them alone. I pray also for those who will believe in me through their message, that all of them may be one, Father, just as you are in me and I am in you. May they also be in us so that the world may believe that you sent me. I have given them the glory that you gave me, that they may be one as we are one: I in them and you in me. May they be brought to complete unity to let the world know that you sent me and have loved them even as you have loved me.'"

(John 17:20–23)

"For you did not receive a spirit that makes you a slave again to fear, but you received the Spirit of sonship. And by him we cry, 'Abba, Father.' The Spirit himself testifies with our spirit that we are God's children. Now if we are children, then we are heirs—heirs of God and co-heirs with Christ, if indeed we share in his sufferings in order that we may also share in his glory."

(Romans 8:15–17)

IN WHOSE NAME?

I chanced one day upon a traveler, worn and weary.
He sat under a roadside awning on a rainy day, dreary.
At first I chose to be slightly cautious and a little bit leery,
But there was something about his person that drew me to him, dearly.

He invited me to come and sit next to him, to my surprise,
But he asked not for bread or coin as a pandering prize.

Silently we sat together for an eternal brief moment of time,
And I could tell he was preoccupied, pondering life's confused rhythm and rhyme.

So I respected his silence and patiently waited for him to first speak,
For I could tell my weary traveler was wise, humble, and meek.

His tattered, threadbare clothes and unstylish shoes
Were evidence he had ventured far in life which had leveled on him unfair dues.

Then my acquaintance finally spoke to me through labored breath, unmeasured,
And what he said I hold more precious than gold or silver, treasured.

"My son, I've journeyed this land and others both far and wide,
Searching even across great salt waters moved by storms and tides.
My excursion's labor taught me to abandon my selfish pride,
And as I approach life's end I've nothing to hide.

So I will tell you now I've come to a firm conclusion,
That any name for Christian's to wear other than Christ is a delusion.

Brick and mortar have names a million above their doors all over the earth,
But the only name early Christians wore was Jesus, in whom we receive eternal
rebirth."

∽

"In the past God spoke to our forefathers through the prophets at many times and in various ways, but in these last days he has spoken to up by his Son, whom he appointed heir of all things, and through whom he made the universe."

(Hebrews 1:1–2)

"The eunuch asked Philip, 'Tell me, please, who is the prophet talking about, himself or someone else?' Then Philip began with that very passage of Scripture and told him the good news about Jesus."

(Acts 8:34–35)

BROTHERHOOD

Brotherhoods in this mortal plane,
Are forged in sweat, toil, suffering, and pain.
Each holds a common purpose in a common name,
Where all who belong prefer to die over disloyalty's gain.

What is it in flesh's life-giving blood
That welds a commitment willing to die where it stood?

Is it DNA, or love that causes abandon's game,
So that death is preferred over disloyalty in a common name?

And yet, even in dying for a shared cause,
Each adherent discovers freedom unequaled in fame or applause.

Truth's answer is found in a bond within each such family,
That makes their brotherly love over hearth and home an anomaly.

And so I pose this question politely and genteel,
Can brick and mortar offer such a sweet deal?

Is it Christ, or variant names of brick and mortar, who died on the cross,
So that souls in the next world would not experience eternal loss?

Hence, may I venture to speak and boldly say
That there's no brotherhood like Christ's under the sun of each day

That offers life, both in this human plane and the holy one to follow,
And being in its fold will lead to the only one hallow.

∼

"For whoever does the will of my Father in heaven is my brother and sister and mother."

(Matthew 12:50)

"Be devoted to one another in brotherly love. Honor one another above yourselves."

(Romans 12:10)

"Now that you have purified yourselves by obeying the truth so that you have sincere love for your brothers, love one another deeply, from the heart."

(I Peter 1:22)

COLD IRON AND ICE

Cold iron and ice,
Cruelly fashioned the ultimate sacrifice.

Cut and hemorrhaged, head and face,
His blood draining and dripping to deface,
Bruised by those calling for His life, extending no grace.

Hands and feet pierced by rusted cold iron, nailed to a tree,
All because, as our lamb, He ransomed our sins to save you and me.

So, what is this ice you speak of on a hot day of torture?
It was the frozen souls of religious hate orchestrating His mortal departure.

Steely eyes, cold souls, rock-solid in their refrigerated glee,
So taken by their successful legal murder they didn't see
That the angel of darkness and his minions were happily dancing excitedly.

Who else but the Christ-child would grow up to fulfill this mission?
No human mind could conceive or design this plan of contrition.

∽

"The next day John saw Jesus coming toward him and said, 'Look,
the Lamb of God, who takes away the sin of the world!'"
(John 1:29)

"For you know that it was not with perishable things such as silver
or gold that you were redeemed from the empty way of life handed
down to you from your forefathers, but with the precious blood of
Christ, a lamb without blemish or defect."
(I Peter 1:18–19)

A HEAVY STONE AND A LINEN CLOTH

A heavy round stone covered the entrance to a cave,
That sealed inside a body—a testimony of how mortals can poorly behave.
Though some of His followers attempted His death to stave,
Others betrayed Him, which led to what some thought was an early grave.

Inside He lay for three days, wrapped in a linen cloth of white,
As death had stolen His life so some felt He had lost his fight.
Then there was suddenly a pure, blinding white light,
And an angel appeared in a dazzling glorious sight.

The stone rolled away as though it was a pebble small,
And Jesus arose from death, defeating Satan to his gall.
The cloth fell away from His body as He stood tall,
And days thereafter He appeared to His followers who at His feet did fall.

There's a unique fellowship of those who believe in the stone and cloth,
And it can only be found in the family who escaped God's wrath.

For it crosses bloodlines, and kith and kin,
And allows a common hope for those who in Him begin again.

So tell me brother about brick and mortar,
Does it have hope in fellowship's charter?

Or did it lie three days, cold and stiff in a rich man's tomb,
Only to rise from the dead to steal eternal gloom?

≈

"Nicodemus brought a mixture of myrrh and aloes, about seventy-five pounds. Taking Jesus' body, the two of them wrapped it, with the spices, in strips of linen. This was in a accordance with Jewish burial customs."

(John 19:39b–40)

"When the Sabbath was over, Mary Magdalene, Mary the mother of James, and Salome bought spices so that they might go to anoint Jesus' body. Very early on the first day of the week, just after sunrise, they were on their way to the tomb and they asked each other, 'Who will roll the stone away from the entrance of the tomb?' But when they looked up, they saw that the stone, which was very large, had been rolled away. As they entered the tomb, they saw a young man dressed in a white robe sitting on the right side, and they were alarmed."

(Mark 16:1–4)

A NAME LIKE NO OTHER

I have been thinking all day,
And I can express it in no other way,

But that in Jesus's name there's no other,
Who can make strangers our brothers.

Because it's in His name alone,
That the lost find a permanent home.

Where else can the loss of this world
Be exchanged for a golden harvest of forgiveness's herald?

But in the one who died on the cross,
So that sins of this world are considered a loss,

Never to be counted or remembered,
By God in whom we pledge our troth, surrendered.

As His creation we have never been our own,
Yet He gives us freedom to choose where we want our eternal home.

So, tell me, please,
In what brick and mortar will we have such blessed ease,

To be forgiven of sin and meet our creator,
Except in the Ecclesia of our maker?

～

"Salvation is found in no one else, for there is no other name under
heaven given to men by which we must be saved."
(Acts 4:12)

JESUS RELIEVES US OF OUR GREATEST FEAR

What is man's greatest fear?
Are there threats that cause the strongest to shed a tear?
Why would an unbeliever suddenly to God draw near?

I believe there is only one meeting common to mankind,
That no matter who he is he fears it most as life unwinds.

It's *death* that does not begin when we are old,
But the spark of life is limited we're told.

Our days are numbered and can't be exceeded,
As God has set each life a limit which is decreed.

What can sooth this knowledge of our final setting sun?
What can assuage our common fear so it can be done?

Brick and mortar have not the answer as the end draws near,
Though many feel safe in its sanctity, drying the eye and comforting the ear.

But brick and mortar will one day return to dust,
So then where will its magic stand, that so many trust?

Our hope and home is found in only the one who died,
And in His death, He averted dying and death's dark tide.

In Him alone we discover peace from our common, human end,
That on the other side of death, to heaven we will ascend.

∾

"There is no fear in love. But perfect love drives out fear, because fear has to do with punishment. The man who fears is not made perfect in love."

(I John 4:18)

"So do not fear, for I am with you; do not be dismayed, for I am our God. I will strengthen you and help you; I will uphold you with my righteous right hand."

(Isaiah 41:10)

"I sought the Lord, and he answered me; he delivered me from all my fears."

(Psalm 34:4)

REST IS WHAT WE SEEK

Rest abiding is what we seek,
Whether headstrong, mild-mannered, or meek.

It's a rest not of laying down or yawning deep,
Nor is it one after a day of toil and harvest reap.

God's human creation seeks a sweet, eternal repose,
As they relax near a cool river in heaven that gently flows.

It will be a rest for bones having come to life's finish, sweetly,
Desirous of a finale to mortal existence because of their noble query.
These bones sought understanding of being, more clearly,
And as age encroached, they appreciated God's wisdom dearly.

Can brick and mortar offer a softer, gentler sleep?
Can it comfort souls seeking repast, deep?
Can it dry tears and embrace to reap
Those who know salvation was not purchased cheap?

No, my friend, only our God in heaven promised,
To offer souls everlasting rest, blessedly honest.

∾

"Come to me, all you who are weary and burdened, and I will give you rest. Take my yoke upon you and learn from me, for I am gentle and humble in heart, and you will find rest for your souls. For my yoke is easy and my burden is light."

(Matthew 11:28–30)

"For if Joshua had given them rest, God would not have spoken later about another day. There remains, then, a Sabbath-rest for the people of God; for anyone who enters God's rest also rests from his own work, just as God did from his. Let us, therefore, make every effort to enter that rest, so that no one will fall by following their example of disobedience."

(Hebrews 4:8–11)

WELLSPRING OF PEACE

Haggard, spent, depleted, bone-dry,
If I continued in this heat without water a moment longer I'd die.

True story is this of a miscalculated, youthful adventure,
Impetuosity didn't count on this excursion being a danger.

African bush scorching in its sultry, equatorial way,
I'll never forget my salvation until my dying day.

Three days without adequate water to drink,
Then found a small spring in a sink hole, my eyes double-blinked.

Nectar of the gods, I thought it was,
Brought from heaven to my lips and tongue because

Gulped, lapped, and inhaled it I did,
Then soothed my parched tongue and sunburned face like a kid.

A peace came over this mortal soul,
Because this essential fluid restored a dying life, making it whole.

A comfort bedazzled my waylaid spirit,
As though I was at peace with all around, far away, and near it.

Intoxicated and addicted to this eternal, momentary pause,
So much so, I didn't want to leave it, for any cause.

Isn't this the peace Jesus has to offer?
No brick or mortar can measure up to it, no matter the size of its coffer.

Let us then gather with those who are sanctified,
To be with Christ in heaven, standing by His side.

~

"My people have committed two sins: They have forsaken me, the spring of living water, and have dug their own cisterns, broken cisterns that cannot hold water."

(Jeremiah 2:13)

"I spread out my hands to you; my soul thirsts for you like a parched land."

(Psalm 143:6)

"As the deer pants for streams of water, so my soul pants for you, O God. My soul thirsts for God, for the living God."

(Psalm 42:1–2)

A PERFECT TEMPLE NOT MADE BY HAND

What temple has been made by man
That's perfected by his hand?

The pharaohs tried it long ago.
Today, though proud, they have somewhat less to show.

King Solomon, the wealthiest monarch of his day,
Spent his great fortune to construct one, but the Romans later had more to say.

Mayans and Incas, where are they now?
No one seems to understand their departure, especially how.

For these and many other kingdoms thought to be perfect, without flaw,
Could not endure time's test in their beauty and what mankind saw.

Their creators and builders stood back in awe,
As the pride and vainglory in their hearts would not thaw.

Yet where are they now?
They are of the dust best suited for the farmer's plow.

So let me tell you of the one-and-only perfect temple.

It was crafted in flesh and blood, flowing free,
While Roman whips on His back brought Him to bended knee.

Its foundation was in wood and iron nail,
Soon to have His side by spear impaled,

Yet His temple arose after a three-day repast,
To live forever outside of time, perfect and vast.

~

"Now we know that if the earthly tent we live in is destroyed, we have a building from God, an eternal house in heaven, not built by human hands."

(II Corinthians 5:1)

"Why do the nations say, 'Where is their God?' Our God is in heaven; he does whatever pleases him. But their idols are silver and gold, made by the hands of men. They have mouths, but cannot speak, eyes, but they cannot see; they have ears, but cannot hear, noses, but they cannot smell; they have hands, but cannot feel, feet, but they cannot walk; nor can they utter a sound with their throats. Those who make them will be like them, and so will all who trust in them."

(Psalm 115:2–8)

WORSHIP OR ENTERTAINMENT?

What draws Christians to a specific assemblage on a Sunday morning?
Is it because each gathering recalls their Savior's life with deep, fervent rejoicing?

Congregations as a whole sing, pray, and have the Holy Scriptures read,
If the preacher is favored, some in the pews may forgo slumber to hear what he
said.

I think this question is answered by a query somewhat inane,
Have those in brotherly association come to worship or be entertained?

No brick and mortar can know an individual worshiper's motive for meeting,
All the brick and mortar can do is provide a worshipful venue for their Sunday
greeting.

However, what uniquely distinguishes a brick and mortar's weekly attendance,
Is if in their get-together their communicants are a congregation or an audience,

Communicants worship, while audiences seek entertainment.
That's why it's so important we venerate the One God sent.

I think this worship objective is easier followed in small groups,
Because there's no corporate policy keeping participants in a political worship loop.

Worship then continues to be what it was intended to be,
A simple time of rejoicing over a Savior who died for you and me.

No choirs, orchestras, bands, lights, pyrotechnics, camera, action,
No YouTube, Facebook, Twitter, or e-mail of a Christian star's latest distraction.

So let us not condemn brick and mortar, because it has its place,
Provided its focus is on our Lord and Savior's face.

∾

"My brothers, as believers in our glorious Lord Jesus Christ, don't show favoritism. Suppose a man comes into your meeting wearing a gold ring and fine cloths, and a poor man in shabby clothes also comes in. If you show special attention to the man wearing fine clothes and say, 'Here's a good seat for you,' but say to the poor man, 'You stand there' or 'Sit on the floor by my feet,' have you not discriminated among yourselves and become judges with evil thoughts?"

(James 2:1–4)

"When you come together, is it not the Lord's Supper you eat, for as you eat, each of you goes ahead without waiting for anybody else. One remains hungry, another gets drunk. Don't you have homes to eat and drink in? Or do you despise the church of God and humiliate those who have nothing?"

(I Corinthians 11:20–22)

"I want men everywhere to lift up holy hands in prayer, without anger or disputing. I also want women to dress modestly, with decency and propriety, not with braided hair or gold or pearls or expensive clothes, but with good deeds, appropriate for women who profess to worship God."

(I Timothy 2:8–9)

CONCLUSION: WHO IS MY FAMILY?

Who is my family?
Such a strange question for me.

Of course the heaven-sent wife I love,
And my beautiful children, sent by God from above.

But pray tell then, what do you mean?
Who else that only flesh and blood could screen?

There are those whom I call sister and brother,
With whom I have a bond like no other.

We are one beyond a building of brick and mortar,
Created on the foundation of Christ by God's divine order.

For those in whose homes we gather to meet and share,
I would sacrifice my life in an instant, without fanfare.

They own my heart and soul in an especially unique way,
Given to them by a Savior who died on a cross, one dark day.

But three days later He arose, defeating Satan and death,
And then gave us a common home with a promise beyond this life's breath.

So yes, I have a family of more than blood, bone, and sinew,
With whom we'll share immortality with a God we on this earth knew.

❧

"Anyone who loves his father or mother more than me is not worthy of me; anyone who loves his son or daughter more than me is not worthy of me; and anyone who does not take his cross and follow me is not worthy of me. Whoever finds his life will lose it, and whoever loses his life for my sake will find it."

(Matthew 10:37–39)

"If anyone comes to me and does not hate his father and mother, his wife and children, his brothers and sisters—yes, even how own life—he cannot be my disciple. And anyone who does not carry his cross and follow me cannot be my disciple."

(Luke 14:26–27)

www.ingramcontent.com/pod-product-compliance
Lightning Source LLC
Chambersburg PA
CBHW061754040426
42447CB00011B/2293